DEAR NIDA

Dear Nida

A Story of Love, Lust & Heartbreak

Brenton Rice

Columbus, Ohio

The views and opinions expressed in this book are solely those of the author and do not reflect the views or opinions of Gatekeeper Press. Gatekeeper Press is not to be held responsible for and expressly disclaims responsibility of the content herein.

Dear Nida: A Story of Love, Lust & Heartbreak

Published by Gatekeeper Press
2167 Stringtown Rd, Suite 109
Columbus, OH 43123-2989
www.GatekeeperPress.com

Copyright © 2022 by Brenton Rice
All rights reserved. Neither this book, nor any parts within it may be sold or reproduced in any form or by any electronic or mechanical means, including information storage and retrieval systems, without permission in writing from the author. The only exception is by a reviewer, who may quote short excerpts in a review.

Illustrations by Bella Solari

Library of Congress Control Number: 2022931175

ISBN (paperback): 9781662924774
eISBN: 9781662924781

Contents

INTRODUCTION

CHAPTER 1
LOVE

CHAPTER 2
LUST

CHAPTER 3
HEARTBREAK

INTRODUCTION

Hello, readers. The following book is comprised of a series of short stories, poems and simple thoughts that capture the essence and presence of who 'Nida' is. The short stories at the beginning of each chapter take you through the journey from the moment I first met Nida to the present day, from my point of view.

So, if you've picked up this book and are wondering, "Who is Nida?"

Well, where should I start?

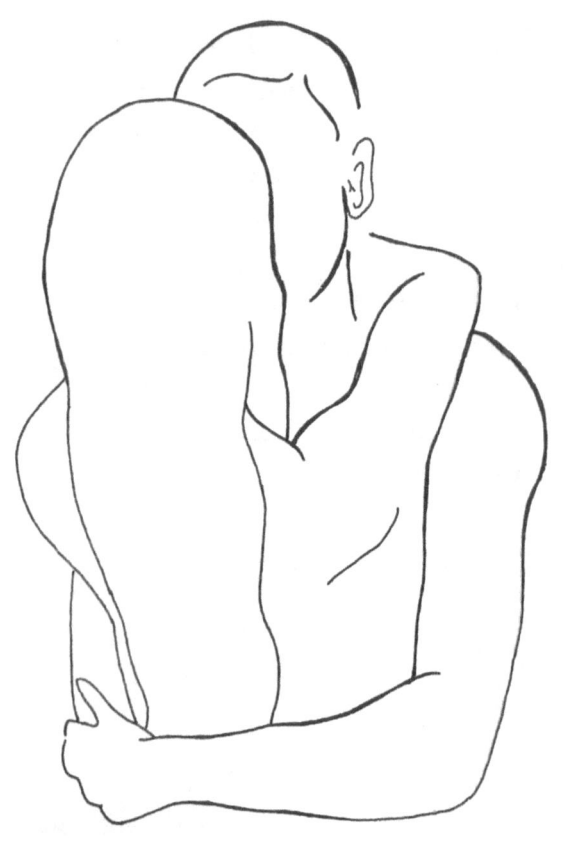

CHAPTER 1

LOVE: A feeling of strong or constant affection for a person

I'll start with the night I met her, one I will never forget. It was a chilly December night in downtown San Francisco, going all the way back to 2015. I was out with some friends and co-workers at the time, and we ended up going to a club. As soon as we walked in, I saw this woman working behind the bar. Later I would learn her name was Nida. *I couldn't take my eyes off her.* She was breathtaking. She had on this tight red dress that showed off her curvy yet slender figure, her dark hair flowing to the middle of her back, eyes that could pierce your soul, and to top it off, her smile was the brightest and most genuine I had ever seen. I knew I was in trouble the moment I laid eyes on her;

so being the shy person I am, I ended up mentioning to another woman working there that I thought the bartender was the most gorgeous woman I had ever seen in my life. She grabbed my arm and said, "Come with me," which is when I was introduced to Nida. I can't begin to tell you how nervous I was, but somehow I managed to get some words out and we chatted for a little bit. I remember telling her that night she was the most gorgeous woman I had ever seen. At the end of our conversation, she ended up writing her number on a napkin, and from that very moment I knew there was something different about her. From that very moment I began to fall. Just how far I'd fall, though, was something I was not prepared for…

Dear Nida

MUSE

She's his muse

His source of inspiration

The reason for these words

And the source of this creation

Brenton Rice

YOUR HELLO

I crave to be in your presence
Yearning for your attention
Mesmerized by your hello
Savoring every last moment

Dear Nida

WHAT SOMEONE LOVES

They say if you want to know what someone loves

That you should look at what they photograph

I have a memory full of your photos…

Brenton Rice

YOU ARE THE ONE

I've never been
So sure
About anything
In my life
You are the one
Worth fighting for

Dear Nida

A SWEET SMILE

A sweet smile

A gentle touch

And a presence filled with grace

He still thinks of her

And when he does

It brings a smile to his face

Brenton Rice

I MISS YOU

I miss you
But I won't tell you

I've told you more
Than I ever should have before

But damn

I miss you

Dear Nida

ROMANCE

You're all the romance I need

Dear Nida

MY ARTISTIC DREAM

Her: follow your artistic dream

Him: you are my artistic dream

Brenton Rice

EVERYTHING

I see you in everything

And

In everything I see you

Dear Nida

ALL

All the words I never spoke

All the words I typed then deleted

All the letters I started

All the paper I crumbled

All the paper in the trash

All the words I've wanted to say

Brenton Rice

FOR YOU AND FOR ME

I wasn't the man
That I needed to be
For you or for me

But I've been growing
Personally
Professionally
Physically
And emotionally

I'm working on myself
I'm not perfect
And will never claim to be
But I promise
To always work on myself
To be the best version
I can be
For you and for me

Dear Nida

I FELL IN LOVE
WITH YOU

I will not fall in love with you

I will not fall in love with you

Fuck.

I fell in love with you

Brenton Rice

AN ANGEL ON EARTH

She makes you feel alive
Like jumping out of a plane
And into the sky
High above
She must've come from
The heavens delivering
An angel on Earth

Taking your breath away
The way her smile
Brightens your day
The clouds making way
For the sun to appear
An angel on Earth

...These feelings sincere

Dear Nida

AUGUST 6th, 2021

She asked me if I remembered
a restaurant that we went to in
Iceland called Sushi Social...

Of course I remember, I responded.
I'll never forget.

I'll never forget any moment that
I've spent with her.

Brenton Rice

ALL I SEE IS YOU

A room full of people
And all I see is you

BIGGEST FEAR

My biggest fear
I think I said it was going blind

I lied…

It's losing you

Brenton Rice

YOUR SMILE

I see your smile in everything

Dear Nida

LET GO

Let go
Let HER go
Is what they say

Move on
They continue to say

So I ask them
Have you ever had a love
worth fighting for?

Brenton Rice

INSIDE AND OUT

You. Are. Beautiful.
Inside and out.

Brenton Rice

GODDESS

In the eyes of the beholder
She's a goddess...

Dear Nida

SPEECHLESS II

My hand is hard to move

It's frozen in time

Thinking of the words

I'd like to say

To put on paper

Thinking of the words

So you could somehow

Grasp this feeling I have for you

Yet, I'm speechless

Brenton Rice

DOES SHE REALIZE

Does she realize
The feelings you get
When you're nervous
Knots in your stomach
Tongue twisted
Stumbling over your words
Not knowing what to say
Or how to say it

You're standing in the presence
Of the woman you love
Wondering if she even knows
How you truly feel
Can she even grasp
The damn feeling
You have for her

Dear Nida

You're nervous

You're excited

You're anxious

You're happy

All at the same time

Does she realize

This is what happens?

Brenton Rice

THE NEXT CHAPTER

He's moving on to the next chapter
of his life, but that doesn't change
how he feels or how often he thinks
of her.

There isn't a morning he wakes up
and doesn't think of her.
There isn't a night that he lays
his head on his pillow and isn't
thinking of her.
There isn't a meal he makes where
he isn't wishing it was her sitting
with him.

There is not a year, not a month,
not a day, not an hour, not a
minute, and not one second that
goes by that he isn't thinking of
her.

Dear Nida

Not. One. Single. Moment.

And no matter what chapter of life he is in, she will always be part of his story...

CHAPTER 2

LUST: A strong desire for something or someone

It felt like love at first sight, but I've heard a saying that goes, "We may love with our hearts, but we lust with our eyes." At the time I first met her, I was trying to get over an ex-girlfriend, and plus I truly thought Nida was out of my league. I tried talking with her but was so nervous, and quite honestly probably didn't come across as all that confident. A few months passed and I learned she moved to New York City, so I started dating someone else, and I now regret how I treated this person, as she was also a sweetheart, but that's for another time and day. Nida and I stayed in touch on and off through texts, as we were living across the country from one another.

Then I moved from SF to LA, then from LA back to Ohio where I am originally from, to spend time with family. During this time, I learned that Nida moved to LA then at some point she moved back to SF, while I moved back to California but this time to San Diego. For whatever reason, our paths never seemed to cross in the same city again.

Fast forward to 2019. I wanted to go on my second trip to Iceland. And there was no one else on Earth I wanted to go with more than Nida. So yes, I invited her. To my astonishment, she said yes and decided to go with me. I couldn't believe it. I was so happy. Now, keep in mind, this trip—an international trip at that—would be the first time that she and I had ever hung out since meeting her that chilly December night in San Francisco…

So…she flew down from SF to SD, and from there she and I flew together to Iceland. Once we landed, we immediately took a regional flight to the northeastern part of the country. We picked up the rental car and started our sightseeing journey. The first day we stopped at these hot baths, which we practically had to ourselves, because it was brand-new and had just opened. As we would move throughout the 'baths' we'd often come close to each other, but I was trying to be a gentleman and not make any moves. But damn, I wanted to kiss her so badly. The first night came and I found myself sitting across the table from the most beautiful woman I had ever seen. At that point in time, there was no doubt in my mind that I was in love—there was no question about it. Later that evening, we finally kissed, and from there the rest of the trip was unbelievable and remarkable.

It is a moment in time I will never be able to erase from my memory.

And from that very moment, I knew it wasn't lust, it was love…

Dear Nida

OCTOBER 18th, 2018

Thinking of you
Across the country
2,000 miles away
Hearing from you once
Just brightens my day

Brenton Rice

OUR SOULS LIVE FREE

What does the future hold?

I don't know
But the world
It's in our hands
Let's live our life
To the absolute fullest
So tell me what you want
And tell me what you need
And I will do my best
To make sure our souls live free

Brenton Rice

STUNNING

Stunning she is
In all her ways
Admiring from afar
He's lost in a gaze

Lost in her eyes
What does he do
Admiring from afar
She has no clue

Stunning she is
He hopes she knows
He's admiring from afar
So let's see how it goes...

IN MY ARMS

I just want to hold you

That's it

Your head resting gently on my shoulder...

You in my arms.

Brenton Rice

WAITING

A deep breath

A deeper sigh

Waiting for a call

Waiting for a text

Waiting for you to say hi

Dear Nida

I WANT TO...

Explore every inch of your body
Lose myself in your mind
Kiss the deepest parts of your soul
And know your innermost thoughts

I want to know...
What makes you smile
What makes you sad
What makes you happy
What makes you mad

I want to know...
Anything and everything your spirit has to offer
The parts of you no man has ever been willing to explore before

I want to...

Brenton Rice

SAY ANYTHING

What are you doing?
Why won't you say hi?
Say something
Say anything

I'm here

Dear Nida

AFRAID

You're terrified to see her, I know
Afraid of the emotions
And the copious feelings

The ones that send goosebumps
Down your spine
Every time you see her

Giving you that same exact feeling
The night you first met her

You're afraid of being speechless, I know
Not knowing what words to say

Afraid of word vomiting every ounce of you

Afraid of what she might say

Afraid if it will make you sad or make your day

Dear Nida

A BIT OF MAGIC

You intrigue me
You interest me
You're a little bit of mystery
A little bit of magic

And I shouldn't be feeling this way

Brenton Rice

SPEECHLESS II

A picture can make me say a
thousand words

But seeing you in person would
make me speechless

Dear Nida

INK ON PAPER

You're like ink on paper
A memory that doesn't fade away
A memory that lasts forever

Dear Nida

LOST AND FOUND

You may be lost
Whether lost in life
Or lost in a moment

You'll find your way
You always do

The only thing is
That it's up to you

Brenton Rice

WHAT IS ART?

Is it words

Is it photos

Is it digital

Is it film

Or is it you?

Dear Nida

ANXIOUSLY WAITING

Anxiously waiting
For just one text
Sitting on the beach
Waiting for what's next

I continue to wait
For you to say something sweet
The moment you do
I'll spring to my feet

You can bring so much joy
It's hard to explain
But when you're silent
It can bring some pain

And that's okay
'Cuz I'll be fine
But to be clear
I want you to be mine

Dear Nida

I WONDER

I wonder what is going through
your mind as you read this

Brenton Rice

I PRAY

I pray
Not for you to be mine
That's a decision only you can make
But I do pray

I pray
That you know where I'm coming from
That you know where I stand

I pray
That you listen to me
That you hear me
That you see me
That you understand me

I pray for you not to be mine
But I do still pray

Brenton Rice

SILENCE

Her silence has never been so loud

Dear Nida

DEVIL'S ACRE

Waiting...

On pins and needles
For you to arrive
Butterflies
Flicker in my stomach
Consuming my mind

The thought of you
Takes over all of me
I'm here
Right in front of you

Waiting...

Do you see?

Brenton Rice

HOLDING YOUR HAND

We're texting back and forth
Holding my phone

As if I was with you
Holding your hand

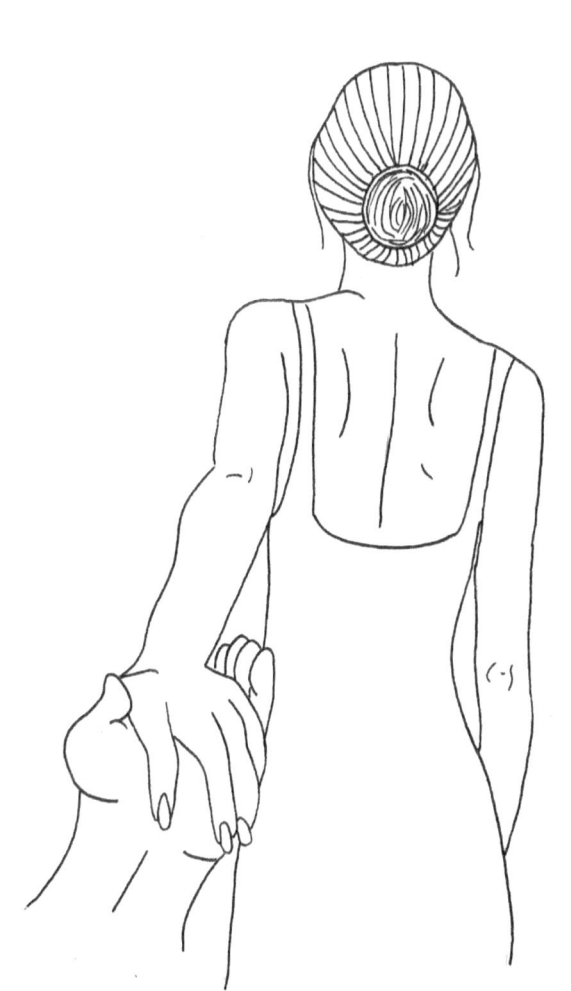

Brenton Rice

DON'T MOVE

I'd hate to see you move
And be so far away again
Farther than you already are

CHAPTER 3

HEARTBREAK: Crushing grief, anguish or distress

On our way back from Iceland we had an overnight layover in Dallas, so we grabbed dinner at the hotel. As we were sitting there, she looked at me and said, "I feel like there's something you want to say to me."

I was like, "What do you mean?"

She responded by saying, "I feel like you want to tell me you love me." And she was absolutely right; I did love her and I did want to tell her, so I did.

We got back from Iceland and continued to see each other. It was difficult, though, because I was in San Diego and she was in San Francisco. I really wanted to make it work, but looking back on it I wasn't a secure man at that point in time. I had insecurities and I let them come through in my own mind, so after a few months I made the decision to want to 'take a break.' I immediately regretted the decision but it was too late, although I continued to try like hell to fight for her. Now, this brings us to the middle of 2020, when one day I randomly checked her Instagram account. When I pulled it up, my heart dropped, shattered in pieces. She had gotten engaged. I couldn't believe it—the woman I had been chasing for years was set to get married to someone other than me. I knew I had to say something, so I sent her a message and congratulated her. Throughout our exchange and from some of the things she was telling me, it seemed like she was unsure if it was the right thing for her or not.

Dear Nida

A couple months went by and we continued talking on and off, as she was working through whatever she was working through. I decided I wanted to fly up to SF to lay it all on the line, and tell her that the man she was planning to marry was not the man that she should marry. Not that I was the right one, but I knew that the one she was engaged to wasn't the right one. I flew up there and we were set to meet at Cupid's Arrow on the Embarcadero. I waited…and waited, but she never showed. She messaged me later, saying she got caught up with work. By that time, my heart was broken all over again, so I ended up sending a text message and laying it all out there. Our communication faded away again. Even though I tried to check in on her to make sure she was doing okay, she wouldn't respond to me.

Another few months passed, which brings us into 2021, and I got a message from her that she had decided to call off the engagement. It wasn't to be with me either, that was for sure, but it was the right thing for her to do after learning what kind of relationship it had turned into. I was upset and sad for her, for the way she was treated by this other person, especially since I had been sitting there wanting to love her with all I have to give. At this point I simply wanted to just be there for her, and I was. I have always dabbled in poetry, but this all sparked me to start putting it down on paper and using a typewriter. So, I ended up putting together a handmade book that I actually hand-sewed together. All of the poems in that book are now in this book. It was July 2021, and I flew up to San Francisco yet again, but this time to give her the book in person and to make sure she knew how I felt, and to let her know that

I was in no need of any type of response or answer.

This brings us to this very moment in time. She and I chat on and off. I know there isn't anything there and that she is still recovering from the bad situation she was in, but for some reason I am still holding on to some sort of hope. But that just continues to lead to more heartbreak...

Brenton Rice

JULY 6th

It's the night before
I can't sleep
Heart beating
Butterflies throughout
I'm nervous
Rehearsing what to say
Can't think of the words

Speechless yet again...

JULY 7th 10:40pm

The time my life changed
You allowed me to be open
To tell you how I feel

No more secrets
No more regrets
I put myself out there
To tell you how much I care

10:40pm—the time my life changed

Dear Nida

JULY 12th

Waiting for your response

Curious to what you have to say

No expectations

Whatever the outcome will be okay

Brenton Rice

ON THE STREETS OF AKUREYI

I lose myself

Looking at photos

Of the past

Mesmerized by the beauty

That you bring to life

So take me back

To the moments

We were chasing waterfalls

And soaking in hot baths

Our naked souls

Running wild

And into the rain

In the middle of the night

On the streets of Akureyi

Not a care in the world

Dear Nida

Two free spirits
Two souls in bliss
One more in love
Than the other…

Brenton Rice

BE PATIENT

Be patient

I tell myself

She's broken

She needs time

She needs space

Be patient

I tell myself

Just be there for her

Dear Nida

I AM HERE

I am here
I'm not going anywhere

So take your time
You need to heal

I am here
I'm not going anywhere

Use my shoulder
To rest your head
Use my ear
I'm here to listen

I am here
I'm not going anywhere

Brenton Rice

SITTING ALONE

At the bar

With my book

Bass bumping

Vibrating my seat

Red wine flowing

The thought of you

Has my mind glowing

Yet I'm sitting alone

With my book

Brenton Rice

THEY ASK

They ask about you

I try to tell my friends that it's all good

I tell them we're just friends, which is true, I promise

But they can see it, and they can hear it, it's in my voice

They know that you mean so much more...

SILENCE II

Your silence has

Never been so loud

A sonic boom

Deep within the soul

Too loud for

Me to bear

Now it's too quiet

For me to even care

Brenton Rice

SHE LOVED HIM NOT

She loved him
She loved him not

Still, he picked the petals of the flower anyway
And he didn't just pick a little, he picked a lot

Hoping that she'd love him

But she did not...

SIGH

A sigh…

There is no relief
Struggling for the words
Struggling for what to say
To capture the thoughts
That consume my entire day

Dear Nida

A THOUSAND GOODBYES

I've said goodbye one thousand times

And I've said hello one thousand and one

Brenton Rice

NOT A PRIORITY

Any other person in their right
mind would have given up long ago

We're texting one minute and the
next I don't hear from you for days

You have no obligation to text me
or respond to me but I don't get it

I've made you a priority in my life
and it's clear that I am so far below
a priority in yours

NOT A PRIORITY II

She proves it over and over
You're not a priority
You're not even on her mind
You've been fighting your ass off
For what?
To be ignored, with no response?
You know if only she understood
That all you're asking for is communication
At the same time, if there is no communication
Take it as a sign
As much as it pains you
To come to that realization
It's a reality you must face
It's not you, it's not her
It's just not the right thing for you or her

Brenton Rice

You can't be mad about that—it's life

And maybe you're not so mad because you're

Stronger than ever before

IF I...

If I stood in front of you
Would you see me?
If I told you I loved you
Would you believe me?

If I called
Would you answer?
If I sent a text
Would you respond?

If I never reached out again
Would you notice?
If I never saw you again
Would you even care?

Brenton Rice

A BEAUTIFUL SUNSET

A beautiful sunset it was
But tonight it just wasn't the same

SHE WAS GONE

He looked up
And there she was

His heart skipped a beat
Shocked by her beauty
Almost fell off his feet

This morning he looked up

And she was gone...

Brenton Rice

YOU WOULDN'T LET HIM

He gave you a kiss
He gave you a hug
He squeezed you tight
Right before your flight
You were here one day
And gone one night
He knew what he wanted
And was ready to fight

But you wouldn't let him...

Brenton Rice

BLINK OF AN EYE

A moment so brief
In the blink of an eye

Before I could say hello
I had to say goodbye...

THAT'S IT...

He lives here
And she lives there

That's it...

Brenton Rice

LOST MY FIRE

I lost my fire
When your flame burned out

Dear Nida

MAKING DINNER

I'm in the middle of making dinner
for myself and all I can think about
is you...

I want you to see it.
I want you to taste it.
I want to send you a picture of it.
I simply wish we were talking.
I wish you were here with me.

But you're not...

Brenton Rice

WATER YOUR SOUL

Let the pain be the rain that waters your soul

Dear Nida

CHASING A GHOST

With each day that passes
And I don't hear from you
It makes things a little more clear

I've been chasing you for awhile
As if I'm chasing a ghost
You're here and then you're not

Brenton Rice

IT HURTS

Hearing the heartbreak

Through the words she types

I get filled with sadness

Knowing she wishes it was different

Knowing she prefers him

Clearly it hurts to hear

I have to be strong

Patiently waiting

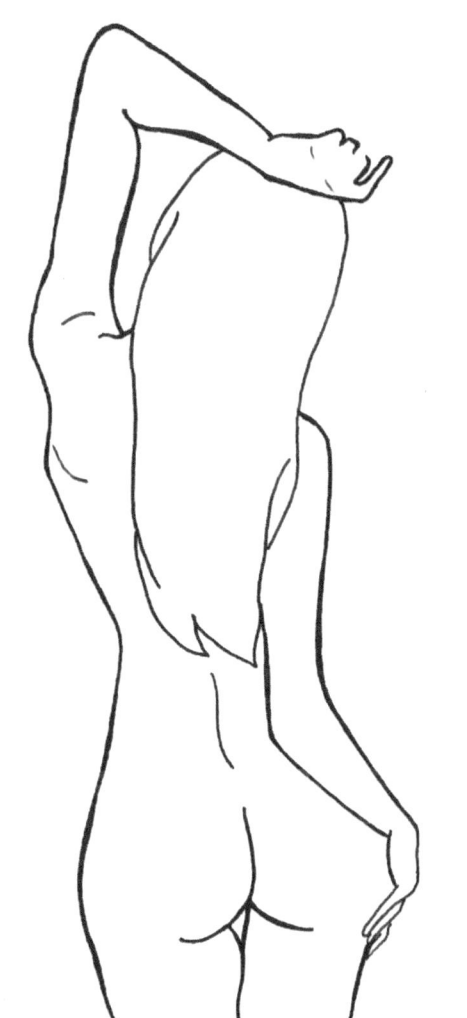

Brenton Rice

SILENCE III

They say a picture speaks a
thousand words

But what does silence say?

Dear Nida

SILENCE IV

You're the photo
That speaks a thousand words
At the same time you're silent

Brenton Rice

MY HEART ACHES

You scream from deep inside
Yet you remain silent
Yearning to help in any way I can
Because I hurt when you hurt
And my heart aches when yours breaks

WAITING FOR YOU

You're here
Then you're not
You disappear
For days on end
Then appear again

And here I am

Waiting for you...

Brenton Rice

A DEEP BREATH

A deep breath
A deep sigh
There is no relief
Struggling for the words
Struggling for what to say
To capture the thoughts
That consume my entire day

Dear Nida

NEW YORK CITY

You said you missed it
You said you wanted to move back

And that destroyed me...

Brenton Rice

MY HEART MY MIND*

They don't stop talking
Yet I exist in silence
Afraid of what might be
Afraid of the violence

The turbulent feeling
That my words may bring
If only I could be open
And let my heart sing

But my pain stays hidden
At the depths of the sea
Deep into my soul
So I just let them be

That's not the way to do it
My mind tells me so
But my heart is in control

And it just tells me no

It's a battle I live with
Each and every day
It can be lonely
But my heart knows no other way

Written 1/20/2017

*THE STORY BEHIND 'MY HEART MY MIND'

This poem was written over five years ago now, and to this day I know exactly why I wrote it.

I wrote it because I wanted to tell you how I felt inside, but at the same time I was terrified. We had never hung out before, but we had always kept in touch from a long distance, and for whatever reason you always made me feel different. You made me feel alive. I could feel every ounce of my burning passion for you. Yet, there was no way I could get the right words together to tell you.

On one hand, my heart wanted to shout out from the rooftops my feelings for you, but my mind was the one saying to be realistic. Doing that will not get you anywhere. So at the end of the day, I would keep things bottled up inside. My heart was telling me one thing and my mind was telling me another.

Side note: I read this poem to her while we were having dinner during our trip to Iceland. I couldn't believe I was sitting in front of her reading it.

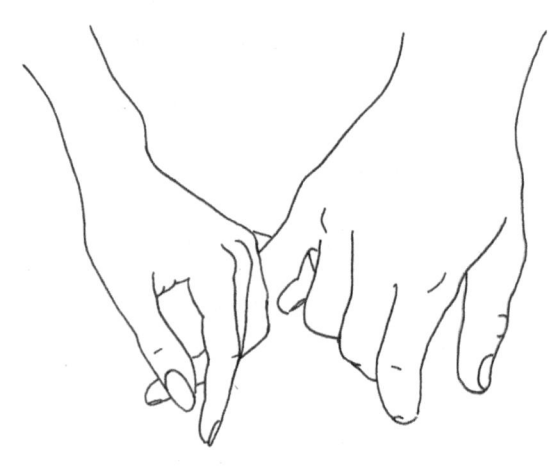

Dear Nida

JULY 12th: UPDATED

You responded...

Now is when I walk away...

Dear Nida,

If and when you ever find yourself reading this, I want to say thank you. Thank you for being an inspiration to me, which has empowered me to accomplish something I never knew I could. Thank you for always letting me express myself to you without judgement. You have no idea how much that has meant to me. It has allowed me to put words on paper, which is something I have always been afraid to do. Thanks to you, I am no longer afraid. So, thank you. Thank you for being such a sweet and gentle soul. I know you have been through a difficult couple of years, and I know we aren't really involved in each other's lives at this point in time; but still, thank you for always being gracious and elegant every step of the way, when you could have shut me out long ago.

With unconditional love,

Brenton

www.ingramcontent.com/pod-product-compliance
Lightning Source LLC
LaVergne TN
LVHW041643060526
838200LV00040B/1697